How to Make Money Online

Selling on EBay

Entrepreneur Series

Saad Ghafoor

Mendon Cottage Books

JD-Biz Publishing

All Rights Reserved

Disclaimer

The information in this book is provided for informational purposes only and it is not intended for use as a substitute for proper financial or legal direction by a qualified financial or legal advisor. The information is believed to be accurate as presented based on research by the author.

The author or publisher is not responsible for financial loss or damage incurred by implementing ideas mentioned in this book. The author or publisher is not responsible for errors or omissions that may exist.

Warning

The Book is for informational purposes only and before starting or running any business, it is recommended that you consult with your financial or legal professional. Always follow all laws and regulations regarding taxes, selling, buying, or ecommerce.

Check out some of the other Entrepreneur Series books
Entrepreneur Series books on Amazon
Check out some of the Science of Living Series books
Science of Living Series on Amazon
Check out some of the Health Learning Series books
Health Learning Series on Amazon

Table of Contents

Introduction

EBay is a good source of income for people like you, who are looking for ways to fund other businesses or just add some income to your family. One thing that makes EBay different is that it is flexible in its nature. It also gives great potential for those serious sellers who want to have a larger amount of monthly online income.

But, as a beginner, EBay is a very practical business venture that you can start with. One good reason for this is that you can earn money even from used items and things that you may think of as garbage in your house. Garbage in the sense that you can find some old items or things that you don't use anymore and you will be surprised that one day somebody will bid on that weird and old stuff in your house. Yeah, that is very possible. So, you can't really tell which item will really give you some bucks. EBay is worth trying and many people fall in love with the process of turning things into cash.

Moreover, there are many surprises that EBay can offer in your entrepreneurial journey. What you need to do is to make up your mind and learn the ways to get started. Selling on EBay does not take a lot of work. The technicalities are so easy to follow and learn. Of course, there are some techniques that can make selling easier and faster.

So, for you to do this, what you need to do is to:

1. Sign up

2. Choose the niches of your products

3. Know where to buy your products

4. Know your competition

5. Know the demand of the product that you are selling

6. Learn how to carefully choose buyer keywords in your listing

7. Learn how to decide the pricing and shipping

8. Learn about the factors to consider when listing your products

All these things will really help you in the EBay business. Knowledge is so powerful when you are using its maximum capacity. And with great entrepreneurial spirit, it is possible that you can earn not only $500 but also more than that amount. Actually, there are a lot of people who make EBay their full time job because they find it very promising.

EBay is a great tool for people who have the passion of selling things for profit. So, if you will use your maximum effort and whole capacity; then it is no doubt that you can join those power sellers on EBay who make thousands of dollars already.

Well, you will never know unless you try. Keep yourself motivated as you continue reading, because you will uncover those eight things that you need to learn in order to know what you are really doing on EBay. Once you have mastered the skills needed for these things, you can make a lot of money on a regular basis.

Chapter 1: Sign Up With EBay

This is the very first thing that you will do. Go directly to EBay.com and sign up. Take note that you can sign up locally because EBay is worldwide, so whatever country you are in, you can always feel at home. Anyway, there's an option that you can sell internationally. So, first you need to click the register button in the upper left side of the site.

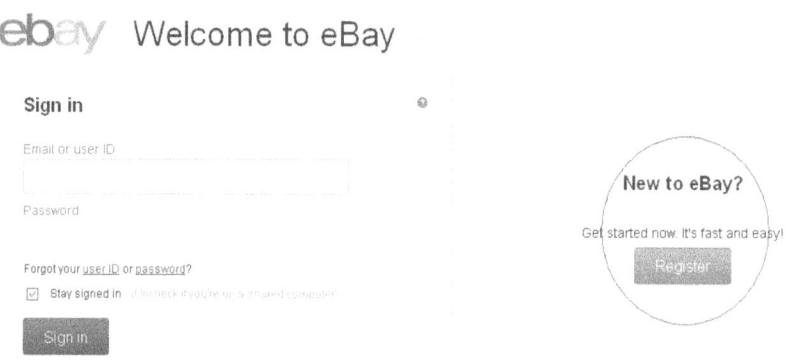

Then you are going to fill the boxes with your complete information. Of course you need an email; you will create a user id, and so on and so forth. This is very basic information that you can easily fill out. But, just be very careful when you are **choosing your user id**. Try to make it relevant to the kind of products that you want to sell. This user id will give an impression towards the customers about you as a seller. Sometimes it can give you a trademark in your business. People will usually remember you easily once your id is related to what you are selling, because they are looking up your products and not to you as a person.

So, keep your username **catchy and easy to read**. In this way people can remember your id on EBay because they sometimes directly find you on EBay as they are looking forward or checking your new items.

Another thing is that you need to read and understand the terms and conditions on EBay. Remember to follow the rules so that your performance rating will not be affected. There are other things too, if you will do, you will be banned from selling on EBay. This usually happens if you don't pay your fees on EBay. These fees will only be applied once you use their tools and other special services, so that your products will be promoted. One example of this is when you are going to feature your product in the front page of the site itself. This will give you the advantage of having tons of viewers to your products. It will also give you a bigger chance of selling your product. So, just be careful in using EBay's tools, because some are not free and some are a little expensive, especially for the starter.

You can take advantage of the tools being offered by EBay, but just make sure that you can cover the amount of money as a profit. Because at the end of the month, EBay will send you a bill and they will give a time frame for you to send your payment. Once you miss payment, your account will be treated as not registered and you cannot sell anymore unless you pay. Yes you can pay late; however, this will affect your rating.

There are still other rules that you need to study, but this one is a little serious because your business will be greatly affected if you can't make your payments.

Chapter 2: Deciding the kind of products to sell

Deciding the kind of product to sell on EBay is quite confusing for starters. But, in the long run, you will know them by having enough experience along the way. To help you not waste your time in doing this, below are the guidelines in choosing the right products to sell.

1. **Choose the product that you are most comfortable with**

   This is a kind of instinctive business strategy for sellers. Once you are selling the things that you are interested in personally, then there's a big tendency that you know your craft. And because you know your craft well, then you can provide not only high quality products but also a high quality service. Aside from that, you will enjoy the whole process because you don't hate the products that you are managing.

2. **Don't concentrate in one product category on EBay**

   In choosing the kind of product, you don't need to choose one category only for your products. Meaning, you can have different kinds of products, but don't choose too many. Just concentrate on 5 to 10 kinds of products to sell. They could be a little related to each other. The reason for this is that some products are too crowded already so you have a lot of competitors. So, you can diversify to have more chances of sales.

3. **Do your research to identify the numbers of your competitors and to identify the demand of your product**

   This part is the most crucial part in selling on EBay. Doing the research is one of the most important things a seller does or else you are simply waiting for your luck on EBay. Knowing the numbers will give you the factual data in order for you to see real earning potential.

First, you need to type the kind of product that you want to sell in the search box of the EBay site. Then, it will show you all the products related to that **keyword**. Now, take note that in the upper portion of the related products, you can see the **total number of products** being listed in that keyword. So, once you can see that there are thousands of products being listed in that particular product, then of course, you have a low chance in earning because the competition is so high.

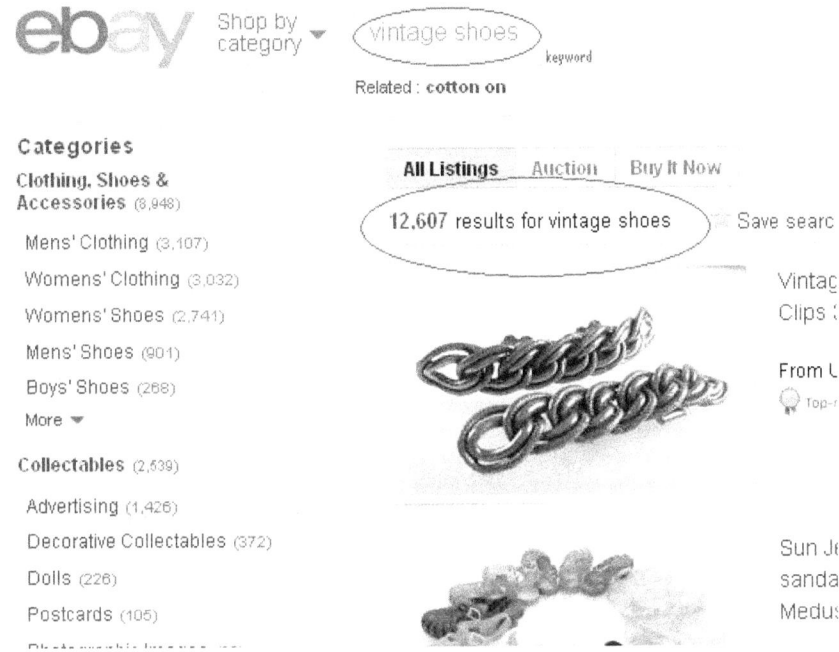

But keep it in mind that you can narrow down your keyword. Meaning, you can make it more specific. For example, enter stuffed toys for kids under 1 year old. After you **click the search box**, you can see your **competitors**. If you can see less than 400 items or lower than that, then of course you have a bigger chance of selling.

The story does not stop there; low competition will be of no use if there isn't enough **demand** for that particular product. In this, you need to focus your attention to your keywords again. **Keywords** are very important in knowing the competition of your product as well as the demand of it. Just make sure that **once you list your item, that keyword should be used.**

So, for you to check the demand of your product, you can use the free tool of Google Adwords. You can use it even without signing in or using your Google account. So, in here, you can type your keyword in the search box. Then, you can even narrow down your research, by choosing the targeted country where you will sell your product. Then after that, you can click in the left side the exact phrase under match types.

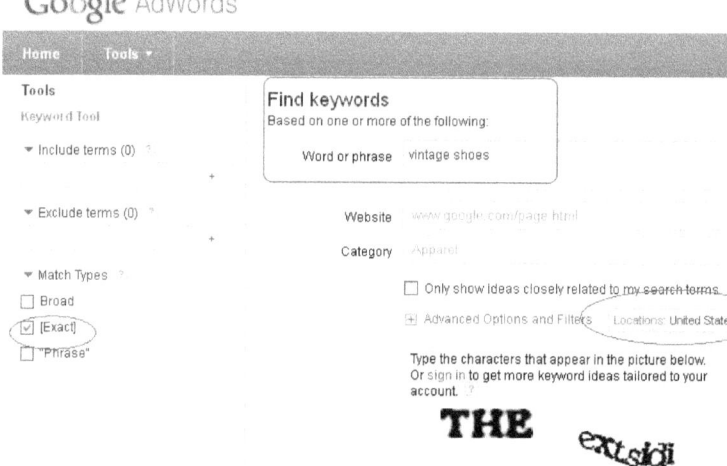

This will help you specifically target the demand base on the specific keyword. Aside from that, you can also type www.ebay.com in the website section and you can add more details if you find it necessary. After everything is clear, **hit the search button and you can see the competition and the demand**. Then you can see the **local monthly searches** that will give you the hint of how many people are looking for that particular product.

			Sorted by Relevance ▾	Columns ▾
☑ Save all **Search terms (1)**			1 - 1 of 1 ▾	
Keyword	Competition	Global Monthly Searches	Local Monthly Searches	
☐ [vintage shoes] ▾	High	8,100	4,400	
☑ Save all **Keyword ideas (100)**			1 - 50 of 100 ▾	›
Keyword	Competition	Global Monthly Searches	Local Monthly Searches	
☐ [vintage shoes] ▾	High	8,100	4,400	
☐ [crown vintage shoes] ▾	High	1,000	1,000	
☐ [vintage style shoes] ▾	High	880	480	
☐ [remix vintage shoes] ▾	Medium	590	320	
☐ [vintage shoes for sale] ▾	High	91	73	
☐ [vintage shoes for women] ▾	High	590	390	
☐ [vintage shoes women] ▾	High	260	170	
☐ [modern vintage shoes] ▾	High	590	390	

So, that is how easy it is. Other people are using more advanced software, but as a starter, you can use this free tool to get started. These are only ways on how to find the exact numbers of things to make sure that you can really sell. Sometimes, you will just be lucky selling on EBay, but most of the time, **you are the one making your own luck**. Do your own research. This will help luck find you.

The Google keyword tool has been replaced since writing this section by the google keyword planner in adwords, but can still be used in a similar fashion to see what products are in demand. Another method I use is to go to Amazon.com and find out what the hot products are and how they are selling and then look for similar products to sell.

Chapter 3: The Best Places to Buy Your Products

When it comes to selling products, you need to consider bright ideas about where to purchase your products to sell on EBay. Sometimes you just need to be very creative and resourceful when it comes to finding nice products that can be sold for high prices. It is always an ideal thing to buy low and sell high. Well, this is very possible if you know where those places are selling affordable products. And also, it is advantageous if you know how to spot these things skillfully.

So, below are the secrets and strategies that you can use wisely in order to earn money on EBay.

1. **Check the old and unused stuff in your house.**

    Well, this should be the first thing that you consider. This is a wise choice for you as a starter. There are many people out there who like buying used products because they are inexpensive. However, these products are selective in the sense that they are already used. So, find things in your house that could be very useful to other people. For example, you have a stroller from your son that you used while he was a child, but now he has outgrown it. You can add this in your listing. And there are a lot more things that you and your family are not using anymore that could still be beneficial to other people.

2. **Go to the flea markets and look cool products**

    Flea markets are the best sources of products which are new yet very affordable. So, do your research for you to find or spot flea markets near your area. You can also have advance knowledge about the best day and time to visit so that you can have find some discounts. You can search through the internet to spot potential deals if you have a smart phone as you are at the market.

    Before going to the flea markets, make sure that you have done your research. You must have done a wide and careful search of different keywords that would give you a high probability of profit. So, you should keep in mind or have a list of those keywords. Then, there in the flea market, take a look for those products related to your keywords. Just make sure that the products are of great quality and are safe to use. You can also talk to the seller to ask for discounts for bulk orders. Most of the time, you can save a lot if you buy in bulk.

3. Look for garage sales

Garage sales are also good sources for expensive items. Most of the time, you can spot some inexpensive things which have great profit potential if sold on EBay. There are greater chances of finding antiques and historical collections at garage sales. Some people don't mind selling the old things thinking that they are worthless. But, for other people who love collecting and investing, old things are valued high. Therefore, do not underestimate garage sales because you can take advantage of it.

4. Visit thrift stores and turn pennies into paper cash

Another great place for digging up some extraordinary products is the thrift store. There in the thrift stores, you can even find branded and not so used products if you are good at finding them. So, be familiar with those great brands that are expensive. Then, check the brand of any product that gets your attention. If you find that it is good yet inexpensive, then go for it. Sometimes, unbranded yet lovely and nice items work best too. So, just try looking around and try analyzing the significance of each item towards the customers' minds. Actually, it is best if you are going to think of yourself as a customer, so that you will have an idea if that item will sell or not.

5. Shop in stores, malls, and other places when there is a sale

It is a common notion that stores and malls are always expensive because the items are new and are in very good condition. However, this is not true at all times. There are days in which huge discounts are offered. And you can take advantage of this. Some sellers are good at spotting inexpensive items in malls even without massive discounts. They are just very keen in spotting nice items like those unsold items, old items, or whatever reason makes the price of the item fall.

6. Find some wholesalers online

As a seller, you can make big profits if you are buying directly from the wholesalers. You can do this online as this is the most accessible way to find new products to resell. Most of the wholesalers who are not that expensive are from China. You can contact them through their website, but just make sure that they are not a scam. Therefore scrutinize their site very well and see their feedbacks through reviews. You can also call or email them and ask more details.

There are still many places where you can find great products for your EBay business. Just try finding items in the most extraordinary way for you to buy low and sell high. Take note that most buyers on EBay want to save, that's why they choose to buy online.

Chapter 4: Deciding on the pricing and shipping costs

As a starter, you are still building a good relationship with your customers, and knowing how to price well is a very good strategy to attract more buyers. You need to remember that the customers are not that ignorant to not know the real cost of the products, because they can see them in stores and malls. Therefore, you need to be very careful in deciding the price.

The most important thing is that you can make money without letting your customers pay too much. But the question is, "How will you do that?" Well, that's another skill to study and master. Actually it's not only the pricing that you should think about, but also the shipping cost. If the customer pays the shipping cost and it is added to the price, you may lose sales and want to put it in the price. So, you need to weigh things very well in order to make lots of sales.

So, to put all these things into order, here are the ways on how to manage pricing and shipping costs when selling on EBay.

1. **Make a profit right after you purchased your item**.

    This might be impossible in your thinking, but for the top entrepreneurs profits are gained once they purchased the item; not when it's sold. Why? Well, this simply means that you should be very careful in your judgment while choosing the items you will sell on EBay. There must be a very high probability that the item will really sell. **So, take a closer look of the item and ask the following to yourself:**

-   Does this item have a great demand in the market? (based on your research)

-   Does it have low competition? (based on your research)

-   Is the quality good for customers?

-   Will I make a profit if I buy at this amount?

- Can the customer afford my markup price for this item?

- Will the customer feel that she can save money if he or she purchases this?

- Or does the item have a great value that makes customer not mind if I raise the price very high?

These are just a few questions that you need to ask yourself. You need to consider the different angles when you are purchasing the product. So, in that way, you made a profit already once you purchase the product; not when it is sold. Because this will only give you the guarantee that you know what you are doing and you are confident about it.

2. Don't be too greedy in pricing.

It is true that selling is an art. But, pricing too high without an appropriate reason is another story. In business, if you are too greedy you will easily fall. Selling is a kind of service. Thus, it must be service oriented. You should not think only of yourself. That is why there is a saying that the customer is always right. Yes, the customer is always right because he or she is just a customer. There's a freedom of the customer to buy or not to buy. And it's a truth that the seller's profit will rely on the customer's decision to buy. Therefore you need to love your customer. Please him or her in the most possible way. Always think about different ways of how to please your customer so that he or she will be coming back to you over and over again. And knowing how to price correctly is the most important factor so that the customer will buy. So, price justly. But there are some times that you can use exemptions for this. Like during holidays or some seasons wherein you can give great importance for a product, especially if there's a limited number for this. In this way, you can raise higher prices because of its significance.

When I was younger my Father owned a clothing store, he would get in a shipment of boots, and they would be of all different styles and designs. He would look at them and he would have paid the same amount for all of them, let's say $50 each for this example. He would mark some of them at just a little over cost at say $60 and then he would take a few of the fancier looking boots and mark them up to $200. I asked him why he did this and he said there are some people who won't buy a $60 boot; they have to have the fancier $200 boot. You need to look at the demand and you will be able to start spotting the Fancier boot as I call it and offer it on your auctions.

3. **Choose your courier well that will suit the customers' shipping cost.**

This is also very important. Sometimes there are inexpensive couriers yet the quality of their service is low. So, your business will also be affected with their performance. **But there's a way that connects to pricing your product.** You can choose a trusted courier with a little less expensive pricing, but you will lower the shipping cost there in your listing. Lowering the shipping cost does not mean that you will be the one to shoulder the excess amount. This only means that you know how to include the shipping cost there in the product's price. So, by this, the customer will not have the feeling of paying too much. So, just learn how to play the tricks in Math by lowering some amounts that will give a good impression to buyers.

4. **Learn when to use auction and buy now options on EBay**

These two ways are the trends when you are selling on EBay. You need to know what products are best to sell for auction and what products will sell best for direct buying. Auctions are good because there's always a big chance that prices will go higher. But, there are many factors for you to consider. Most of the time auction products have higher value and higher demand. If you purchase the item at a very low price, but the value is expensive, then auction it. The possibilities are endless. But sometimes, it depends on your motive. If you want to make quick cash, you can also use a buy now button with your desired price. But many are saying that the buy now button scares buyers. So, be careful when doing this. The buy now option is only good for inexpensive products and also expensive products yet with very high quality.

Pricing and shipping costs are mostly related to each other. And when you are considering your prices you need to think about all the other factors like what are being stressed above. But the longer you spend time with EBay you will know and learn different ways in order to make things work. Just don't be afraid to fail. Try using different tools and ways in order to prove what will work best. There are many sellers who found their own formula in making huge sales on EBay. And one day, you can be one of them.

5. Make your own promo and other tricks.

Just like other stores and businesses, promos and discounts are great marketing strategies. You can do it too in your listings. Give your viewers the hint and the announcements of promos and some discounts. You can even think of your very own tricks about promos and discounts so that you can attract more buyers. Sometimes you can offer buy 1 take 1, 10% discounts, and free shipping promos. So, it's up to you. Also combine products to give a higher perceived value.

There are still many other ways of improving your listing to make it outstanding to buyers. Just take note that you are selling personally in your listing; therefore sell best by convincing them that your product is really good.

6. Register with PayPal

PayPal is the number one method people use to accept payment from EBay auctions. If you don't have an account, go to http://PayPal.com and set up an account to be able to accept payments from your sales.

Chapter 5: The Factors to Consider When Listing Your Products

When you are going to list your products on EBay, there are things that you need to keep in mind. A good looking listing does not only mean being attractive to the eyes of the customers. There are still other important factors than that. The entire listing should showcase all the necessary things that a customer may need as he or she goes through the specifications. The overall appeal must not be too hard in selling or else the customer will be scared away.

So, in order for you to make this, the following will help you in making your listing a stand out listing among the crowd.

1. **Have a clear and presentable picture of your product**

    This is maybe the most common advice to new sellers on EBay and actually it is really true. Spending more time taking nice pictures will help you boost your sales. If you know how to use Photoshop and other software like that, then that would be better. Whether you like it or not, people like pictures. And this is the most important item in your listing that can grab the attention of buyers. Another thing is that the picture must honestly show the real quality and status. Don't trick the customers or else they will give you a very low feedback after they get the product.

2. **Write the details and specifications of your product in an organized way.**

    This time you need to make a balance in the overall look of your listing. The **colors must be in harmony with each other** and must not be hard to look at. Actually, you can use some free templates to change the skin of your listing into a more professional look. Even if you don't do this, you can use your very own creativity to create a simple look. After that, make sure that all the **details** like colors, brand, measurements, and other things are **exact**. The sizes and measurements are very important. But most of the time, the complexity of writing the details depends upon the kind of product that you are listing. So, just make sure to cover all the necessary information for your customer. Actually, even if your product has some flaws, you need to be specific about the flaws and be honest to your customers. Aside from that, choose your **keywords** well and **place your product under the right category** so that it will be easier to find by the buyers when searching.

3. **Observe the most appropriate time for your listing to start and end.**

This is a kind of a strategy for you to make sure that buyers have enough free time to browse on the internet in order to see your products. So, you need to observe the peak hours in which there are thousands of people online on EBay. So, most of the time, these are a few hours after lunch, after work in the afternoon, after dinner time, and also during the weekends. Make sure to start your listing during peak hours and also end your listing during peak hours, like weekends, in order to allow more viewers to see your listings. This strategy is really very helpful for you to have more sales from EBay.

Making a listing takes time and effort at first. But, after you master the skills, you will know how to make your business mechanical. Once you have mastered the whole process, you can make things easier for you by systematizing things. Actually, you can use a lot of software to save time especially if you list in bulk. Don't be too much of a hurry. Take your time as you are going to learn more about the ways in making a standalone listing.

Conclusion

Selling on EBay makes you feel and think that you are really an entrepreneur. You can feel your very own freedom and you can use the most of your free time. EBay gives you your desired working time and will give enough time to rest while waiting for the ending of your auction. In this case, business is easier to manage.

However, just like any other business, you need to manage it well in order to grow. You should set a specific amount of time every day for you to reply to inquiries thru mails or text messages. Sometimes, customers may call you directly, but it is your option to have it set so it will work best for you.

Sometimes, you need to edit some mistakes in your listing and you need to take care of your stocks. You need to clean them for them to be presentable and ready to ship. Other stuff needs to be washed and cleaned so that they will smell good too.

Overall, it takes common sense in order to succeed on EBay. All these things are basic information only for you to get started. But keep mind, this is very powerful advice for you to follow in order to make a start. The most important things are your keyword research, quality of the product, high probability of profit, great listing, and remarkable customer service.

And most of all, you need to treat this EBay business professionally because it will pay you back greatly. The earning potential on EBay is not only $500 a month. You can earn more than that. But of course, you need to work harder.

It may be difficult for you to get started, but just try one step at a time. If you are convinced that you want to do it then there's no problem in it. Just go for it and keep on pushing yourself to go to the next level. Then enjoy the whole process, everything will get easier and faster for you as you do it more often. Once you receive your first payment from your first customer then you can really prove that EBay truly works. After that, business will simply go on while you are funding your other businesses or ideas.

Author Bio

Saad Ghafoor

Education
Bachelors, Human Resource Management University of the Punjab
2010 - Present
High School, Computer Sciences Forman Christian College
2008 - 2010

Check out some of the other JD-Biz Publishing books
Health Learning Series

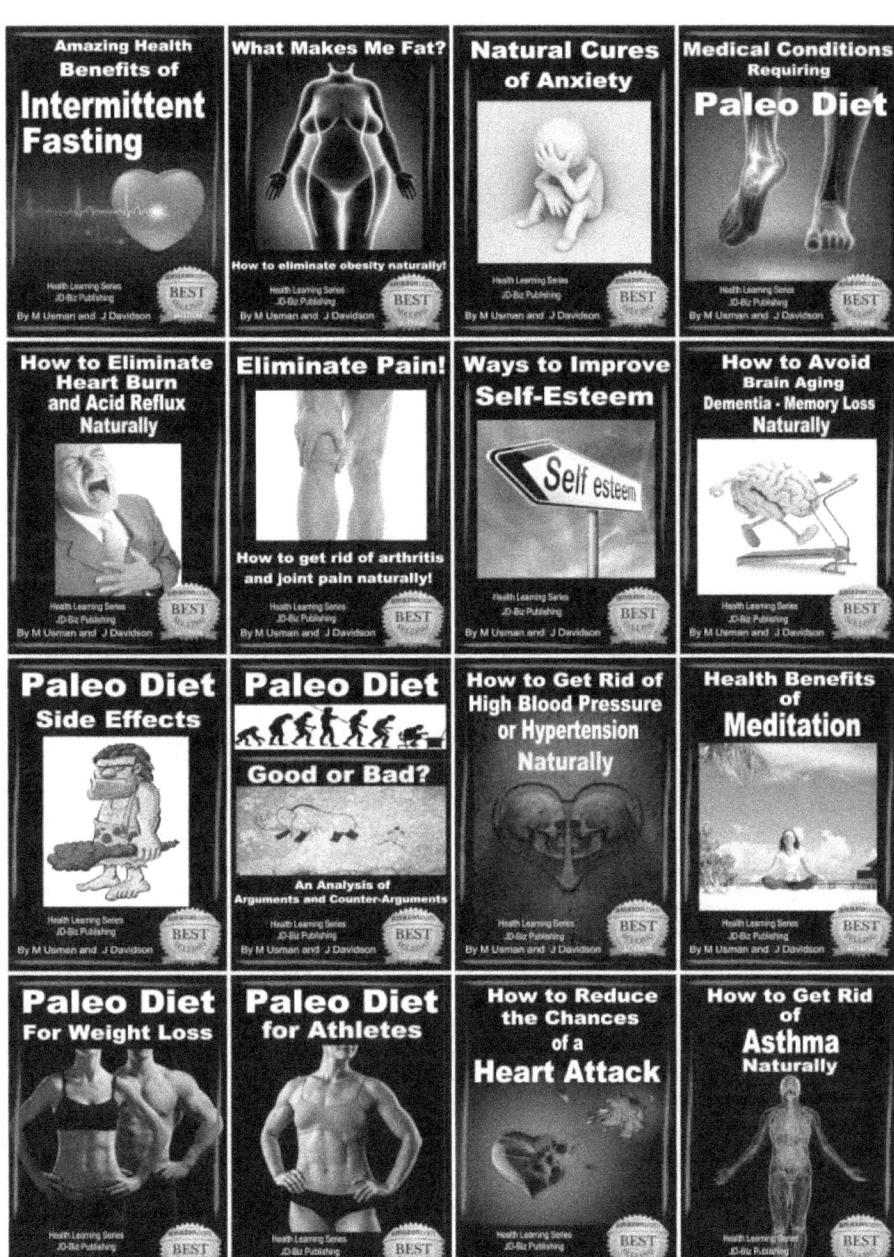

Amazing Animal Book Series

Learn To Draw Series

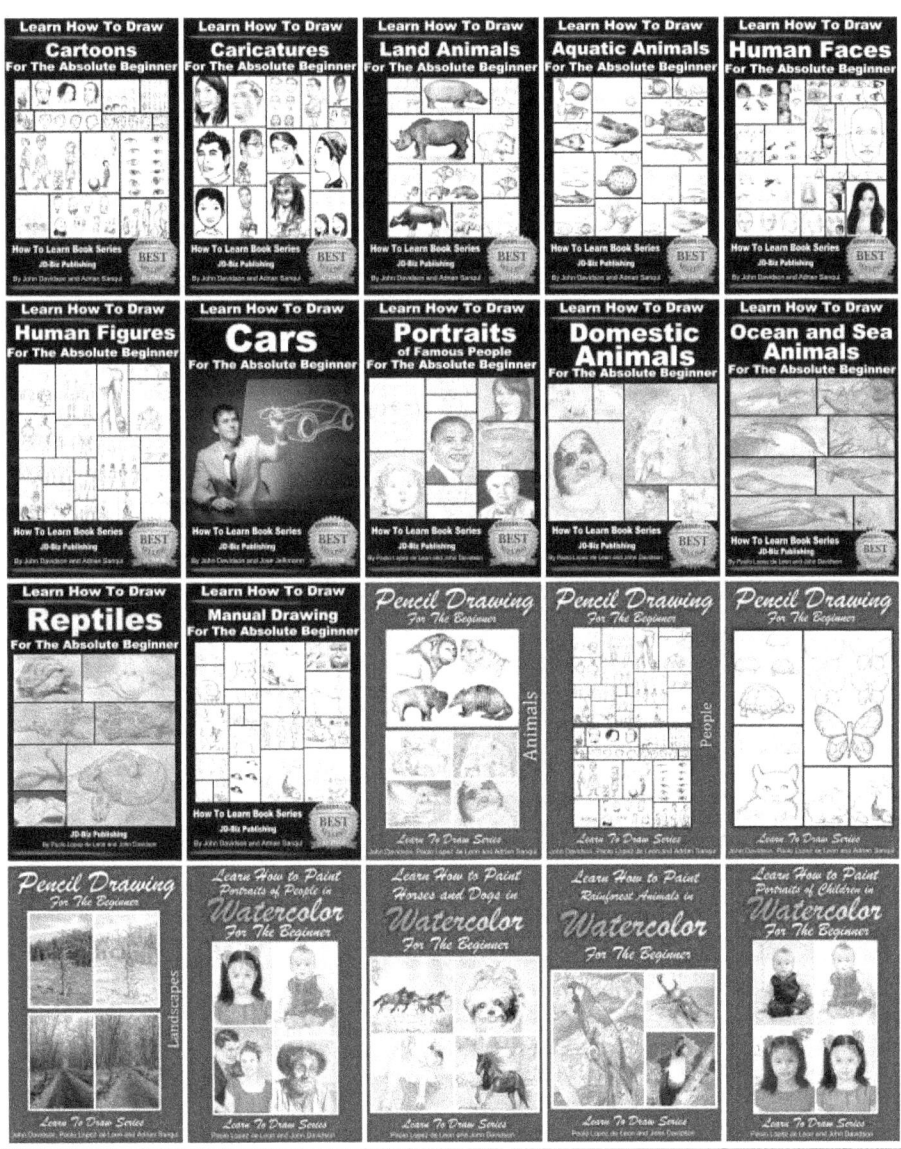

How to Build and Plan Books

Entrepreneur Book Series

Publisher

JD-Biz Corp

P O Box 374

Mendon, Utah 84325

http://www.jd-biz.com/

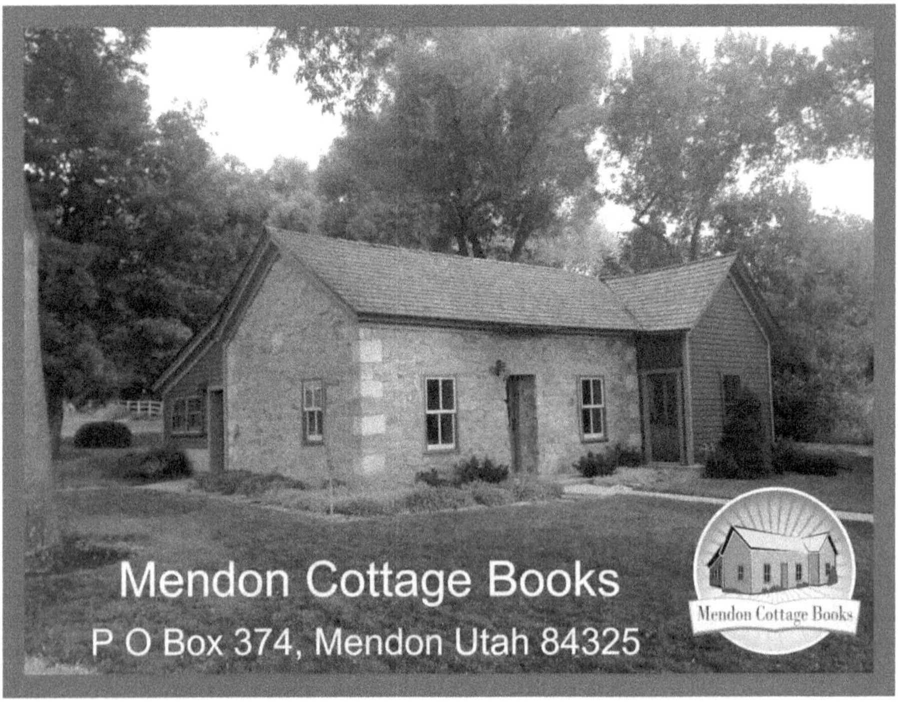

Mendon Cottage Books

P O Box 374, Mendon Utah 84325

Mendon Cottage Books

www.ingramcontent.com/pod-product-compliance
Lightning Source LLC
Chambersburg PA
CBHW070756180526
45168CB00004B/1637